American Indian
Art and Culture

TIGUA

Heather Kissock and Jordan McGill

WEIGL PUBLISHERS INC.
"Creating Inspired Learning"
www.weigl.com

Published by Weigl Publishers Inc.
350 5th Avenue, 59th Floor
New York, NY 10118

Website: www.weigl.com

Library of Congress Cataloging-in-Publication Data

Kissock, Heather.
 Tigua : American Indian art and culture / Heather Kissock and Jordan McGill.
    p. cm.
 Includes index.
 ISBN 978-1-60596-982-4 (hardcover : alk. paper) -- ISBN 978-1-60596-983-1 (softcover : alk. paper) -- ISBN 978-1-60596-984-8 (e-book)
 1. Tiwa art--Juvenile literature. 2. Tiwa Indians--Material culture--Juvenile literature. 3. Tiwa Indians--Social life and customs--Juvenile literature. I. McGill, Jordan. II. Title.
 E99.T52K57 2011
 305.897'496--dc22

                              2010005355

Printed in the United States of America in North Mankato, Minnesota
1 2 3 4 5 6 7 8 9 0 14 13 12 11 10

042010
WEP264000

Photograph and Text Credits
Cover: Alamy; Alamy: pages 6, 7, 9T, 16, 17T; Corbis: pages 4, 12B, 14; Getty Images: pages 5, 10, 11, 15, 22, 23; Nativestock: pages 8, 9M, 9B, 12T, 13, 17B, 20, 21.

PROJECT COORDINATOR Heather Kissock

DESIGN Terry Paulhus

ILLUSTRATOR Martha Jablonski-Jones

Contents

The People

The Tigua Indians live in the northern part of Texas, near the New Mexico border. They belong to the Pueblo Indian group, whose **traditional** lands covered much of the dry **semi-desert** areas of the southwest United States. The Tigua are the only Pueblo Indians living in Texas.

Today, most Tigua live on a **reservation** near El Paso. There are about 1,500 members of this Indian tribe.

NET LINK

Find out more about the Tigua at **www.texasindians.com/tigua.htm**.

Tigua Homes

PUEBLOS
Like most Pueblo Indians, the Tigua lived in pueblos. These houses were like apartment buildings. Each family had its own set of rooms inside the pueblo.

Pueblos were made mainly from mud. Mud bricks were used to create the walls. Logs were laid across the top of the building to form the roof.

Tigua Clothing

MEN'S CLOTHING

In the past, Tigua men wore a **breechcloth** that covered them below the waist. The men went shirtless on top. They would cover themselves with a cloak in cold weather. When Europeans arrived, Tigua men began wearing shirts and pants.

WOMEN'S CLOTHING

Tigua women wore knee-length dresses called mantas. They draped over one shoulder, leaving the other bare. Later, the women began to wear a blouse underneath the manta.

HEADWEAR

Tigua men often tied cloth headbands around the top of their head. They sometimes wore fancy headdresses made from bison fur for ceremonies.

JEWELRY

The Tigua wore jewelry, such as necklaces and bracelets. Jewelry was made from silver and a blue stone called turquoise.

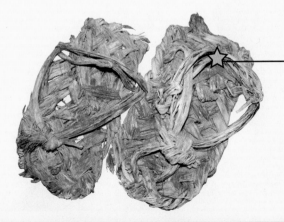

MOCCASINS AND SANDALS

Both men and women wore deerskin moccasins on their feet. In the summer, they wore sandals made from **yucca** plants.

Hunting and Gathering

DEER

Deer roamed Tigua traditional lands. The Tigua hunted them for food and clothing.

BISON

The Tigua hunted bison for food. They also used bison to make tools and clothing.

CORN

Corn was the Tigua's main crop. The Tigua would make bread and **tortillas** from ground corn.

The Tigua farmed much of their food. Growing crops made them settle in one area and form villages. The Tigua also hunted animals and gathered plants found in nature.

HERBS

The Tigua gathered herbs to heal different illnesses. They used rosemary to heal an upset stomach.

BEANS

Beans were another important Tigua crop. Green beans were used in stews and other dishes.

SQUASH

Squash was a common Tigua crop. The Tigua often fried squash with other vegetables.

Tigua Tools

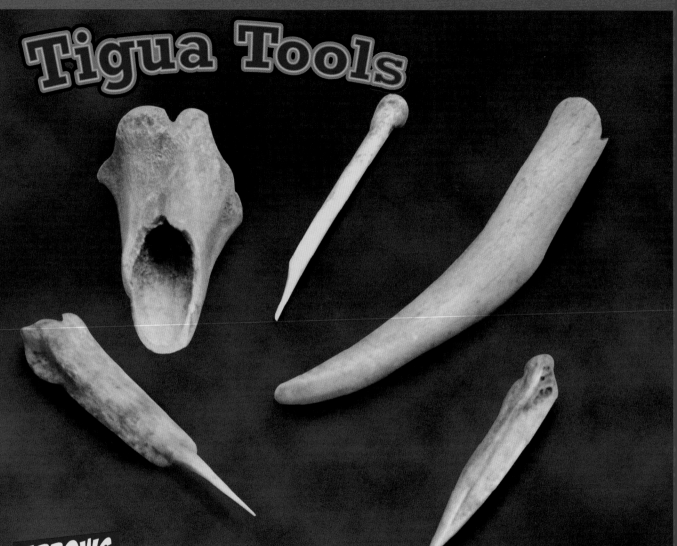

ARROWS

The Tigua made tools such as hoes and arrows. They would use wood to make tool handles. The heads of their tools were made from bone or rock.

Tigua Ideas

The Tigua would use the metate and mano to crush minerals into a fine powder. The powder was used to make paint.

METATE AND MANO

The Tigua used a metate and mano to grind corn and other seeds. The metate was a large bowl-shaped rock. The mano was a small rock that could be pushed around inside the larger rock.

Moving from Place to Place

WALKING In the past, the Tigua traveled by foot much of the time. Some Tigua used walking sticks to help them on their journey.

TRAVOIS

When moving objects from place to place, the Tigua used a travois. A travois was a type of sled. It was made up of two poles that were joined by a small platform. Items were carried on the platform.

Tigua Music and Dance

DANCE

Dancing was an important part of Tigua **culture**. The Tigua danced to honor people, animals, and events that made up their daily life. The Buffalo Dance was performed before the Tigua began hunting to encourage a successful day.

NET LINK

Learn more about the Buffalo Dance at www.aaanativearts.com/article150.html.

DRUMS

Drums often accompanied dancers. The frame of the drum was made from trees. An animal skin was stretched across the frame. When the Tigua hit the skin with their hand or a **mallet**, it produced a sound. Sometimes, rattles were used to create sound as well.

Deer Hunter and White Corn Maiden

Long ago, the village of San Juan was home to two very gifted people. The man, Deer Hunter, was an excellent hunter. He often supplied the entire village with food. The woman, White Corn Maiden, was very skilled at making pots and clothing for the villagers.

Over time, the man and woman fell in love. They stopped hunting and making items for the villagers. The villagers asked the couple for help, but they were too much in love. They ignored the villagers' requests.

Suddenly, White Corn Maiden became very ill and died. Deer Hunter refused to believe that she was gone. He walked all over the village trying to find her. Finally, he found her spirit and asked her to return with him to the village. She did, even though she knew the gods would be angry.

The couple was happy, but soon, one of the gods came to Earth. He told the two that their need to be together was selfish. As punishment, he sent both of them to the sky, where they now shine together as two stars.

Tigua Art

POTTERY

Pueblo artists, including the Tigua, were known for their pottery. To make pottery, artists cleaned clay before shaping it into a bowl or container. Then, they baked the clay until it was hard. The Tigua painted the pottery with dyes made from plants.

BASKETS

Pueblo Indians made baskets as well. They used local plants, such as yucca, willow, and sumac, to make these containers. The baskets could be woven or coiled.

Stovetop Corn Bread

Ingredients

1 cup yellow
    cornmeal
1/2 cup buttermilk
1 egg
4 slices crumbled
    bacon

1 teaspoon sugar
1/2 teaspoon
    baking soda
1 teaspoon salt
1 tablespoon
    bacon drippings

Instructions

1. Mix dry ingredients in a bowl.
2. Beat the buttermilk and egg together. Stir into the cornmeal mix until well moistened.
3. With an adult's help, heat the bacon drippings in the skillet.
4. Pour the batter into the skillet.
5. Cover, and let bake for 10 minutes over low heat.
6. Turn the batter over, and bake the other side for 10 minutes until the center is firm.
7. Serve in wedges while still hot.

Glossary

breechcloth: a cloth that covers the lower part of the body

culture: the arts, beliefs, and habits that make up a community, people, or country

mallet: a light hammer used to play a percussion instrument, such as a drum

reservation: land set aside by the government for American Indians

semi-desert: an extremely dry area that is known for having sparse vegetation

tortillas: thin, round, flat breads

traditional: relating to beliefs, practices, and objects that have been passed down from one generation to the next

yucca: a type of evergreen plant found in warm parts of North America

Index